For my daughter, who's been through it all with me and has been my biggest inspiration.

And my older sister, who believes in me and guides me through some of my rainiest days.

glow up [gloh up]

Verb (used without object)

To go from the bottom to the top to the point of disbelief. An incredible transformation.

Table Of Contents

Prologue

Growing up is hard, I thought I had done all the growing up I could do by 25, but once I stumbled upon my 30's I realized holy shit... I still have no clue. There's still so much I don't know a damn thing about. And each chapter of this large and beautiful life we have, is going to demand a new version of us. We're constantly having to adapt, but let's be honest, we. are. all. ill-prepared. I mean, sometimes we don't adapt at all! The next chapter of life begins and we don't seem to be able to evolve towards it. Well, the purpose of this book is for personal growth, to help steer you in the right direction towards being the best version of you. The version of you that's a chameleon who can confidently take on challenging mindsets, situations, and relationships in each demanding season of life. That's what glow up is all about, going through an incredible transformation to your best self. But before any of that can take place, I am going to encourage you to face some things about yourself and to take accountability first, to get there.

Face yourself and take accountability, are you conscious and aware of all the things that don't serve you right now? Maybe too much time has passed, that we've reached a point where we've begun to accept our miserable situations, we became *okay with it.* It can be scary, but it's important to take the time to snap out of it- to ask ourselves this question. Does this serve me? I don't care what it is, think about it. If you don't like your relationship, why aren't you changing it? You don't like your friendships, why do you still hang out with those people? You hate your job and feel like you're in a rut, but your ass is still working there isn't it?! You're still walking through those doors Monday through Friday! It seems so obvious that we should make changes once something makes us unhappy or no longer serve us, yet none of us are making moves! It is because we need to be real about what's going on, we need to be conscious to realize what it is exactly we aren't happy with. That's what it looks like to face yourself and be accountable.

I challenge you to take pause, to wake up and be present. To be truthful about what's going to better you and what slows you down right now. This needs to happen, for you to change from your bullshit. I'll give you this, perhaps you were aware that you've been suffering all the symptoms of unhappiness, but you hadn't had reason enough to make the necessary changes or you don't know how to. Either way, we're here to Glow Up, to transform ourselves to the point of disbelief. Channel that inner consciousness now, so that you can realize what holds you back from making the right moves. This is what opens you up for change, to take back control and reprioritize, so you can live your best life going forward. You are an ongoing project, project you! Once you find what works, it's a rinse and repeat system, a constant do-over, again and again. A practice. Because the moment you begin listening to yourself, you take care of yourself and everything changes, everything falls into place and the world gets to experience the best version of you too. You deserve it!

This is what it looked like for me, I had an emotional meltdown one Tuesday evening, pulling into my garage. At the age of 32, I was feeling lost, asking myself "Why does it seem, for some reason, that things have always been harder for me?" This is where I took a pause and gained consciousness to sort through it. My whole life, certain tasks and life milestones have been such an ordeal for me to obtain. Whereas seemingly for everyone else, it was effortless. I see others, who had an easier time buying their house, women who had dates lining up out the door, people who go paleo and are in amazing shape, freelancers who have found a way to make a stable income. Now let's describe me, a single mom to a 15 yr old, barely scraping by with the bills. A woman who committed 6 years to earn a Master's degree while working full-time, only to end up getting way below her pay grade at a large company. Barely made it to getting approved for a loan on a townhouse, a serial dieter always looking for the next diet program... A blogger and writer, begging for the next writing opportunity. It's as if I always chose the winding more complicated path over others around me, who appear more at ease from start to finish.

The point was I was unhappy. Now it doesn't mean I was unhappy with my degree, my job, my weight or my success as a writer. It was deeper than that, I was unhappy that it seemed like I always had to work harder for it. It almost felt like, I wasn't supposed to have it, because I had to jump hurdles. I never felt accomplished or like I was doing a good job. More importantly when I dug even deeper, I realized what was most problematic, was the way *I viewed things.* This is what made me most miserable of all! Those were my layers, I unpeeled and unpeeled until I found the things that weren't serving me. I wasn't feeling myself, I was SICK of myself, but either way, I no longer wanted to be a victim. I no longer wanted to compromise those around me over it and I didn't want to lose myself. Lastly, I had issues letting go of things from my past that no longer served me, I was stuck and unable to adapt to the new seasons in my life which demanded a newer and stronger version of me. It was time to snap out of it, pull my big girl panties up and glow the hell up.

This book isn't my pity party, it's an invitation to change. You're not entitled, don't give me that Millenial bs, you're *deserving*, we all deserve it. We only live and die once! So who says the next guy deserves to live their best life over you? Facing yourself and taking accountability will look different for everyone, but all will be equally important for change to take place. Now I get it, I don't know you, but I want you to unpeel your layers too and if at the end of the day I can at the very least have one person make positive changes for themselves through this book, then I'll consider it a success. I am not a doctor or a motivational speaker, but I'm a real woman who went through this and found that being aware, owning up and unpacking my shit, is the process that helped me discover just what changes needed to be made. To ultimately become that confident chameleon that could take on anything that comes next! I want to share this, in hopes that it can help you too. We're in this together, so mark this day as day one, the day you shift your mindset or the day you confirmed some of the things you knew all along. Maybe this could even be… the day you just became better. Better from whatever is harming your lovely spirit. It's time to look after *you* and to take charge of being your most amazing self for all the world to see! Come on, we're in this shit together, you can do this.

Chapter 1

Be Fearless

"Doubt kills more dreams than
failure ever will."
-Suzy Kassem

What are you afraid of? You may not be fully conscious of this, but fear likely shaped a lot of the biggest decisions you made in your life. Where you are right now, is the result of the fears you had, fears that caused you to make the decisions you made in the past- Your current life, is now the result! You're probably thinking, who the hell does this woman think she is?! But be completely honest with yourself, look at where you are right now. If you're in a relationship with someone who mistreats you, you are afraid of what's going to happen if you leave, so you stay. You are in a job that undervalues you, but you are afraid you won't find anything else, so you stay. You never asked your crush out, they're with someone else now. A new position at work became open, but you never applied, so the straight out-of-college grad got it instead. Fear is a powerful thing, not only did it make up where we are now, but it also threatens our future! Say you're an artist, but putting yourself out there means opening up to criticism. You're afraid that they'll see you as an amateur, there's too much at stake, so what do you do? The dream comes to a screeching halt and you *never* put it out there! Because of fear, people will put off their dreams until next year, then another year after that, each year of putting it off turns into putting it off for the rest of their lives. Just as the quote by Suzy Kassem suggests, it's the doubt that is killing your dreams rather than the actual failure itself. You created doubt that you're ever going to make it and that ruined everything for you before you even tried and what a shame!

You Don't Know Until You Do It

Fears can be a self-sabotaging tool, we don't mean for them to be nor are we aware of it at the time. But in life, you must take a pause and step back to look at situations. Am I doing this out of fear? Let's unravel this a little further, in all these scenarios I mentioned about being afraid... You're making an assumption, you've already decided in your mind that leaving the bad spouse means you're alone forever. You already decided that if you quit, you're entirely jobless and there's nothing else out there for you. You decided that if you apply for that new position, you aren't good enough to get it. You decided that your crush would never be with someone like you, if you were the last person on earth. Finally, you already decided that everyone's going to hate your art and you are going to be humiliated! But, how do you know 100% for certain, those are the results? You don't right? The only way you know the result, is if you do them! We are all disadvantaged, because we don't know the outcome of anything. So let me dare to say, your assumptions... could be wrong! What if leaving the toxic relationship, leads both of you to more loving and compatible partners with other people? Or perhaps you get the job that you thought you were underqualified for?

So how silly is it then, that you've allowed fear to dominate your decisions one way, based on the assumptions of the results, that you can't even be certain about in the first place?! Sorry to break it to you, but your superpower is not to predict the future. None of us can! But with this understanding, shoot, you might as well have taken the risks! Am I saying to throw all caution to the wind, that everyone should quit their jobs and divorce their significant others? Not necessarily, but this is about knowing *your truth* about your life situations. We should treat fear more appropriately. When we apply it to the right analogies, fear means don't touch the flame, because you'll burn yourself. Don't put your keys in the electrical outlet or you'll electrocute yourself. Don't dive into a 10-foot pool if you don't know how to swim, you'll drown. These are proven results that we can appropriately be afraid of. But when it comes to matters of the heart, the relationships we have, experiences that we crave and our life passions, we cannot let fear decide for us! If nothing else, *be fearless in the pursuit of what sets your soul on fire*.

Listen to the Messages

A quote by Will Smith, "Fear is not real. It is a product of thoughts you create. Do not misunderstand me. Danger is very real. But fear is a choice."

There's an excellent story Will Smith gave about his skydiving experience and fear. When I listened to it, it sparked something within me to have an *Ah-Ha!* Moment.

He describes the scenario of when he committed to skydiving in Dubai. He agreed to this idea and the night before the jump, he spent all night unable to sleep, stressed and afraid. The next morning it wasn't any better, he was freaking out. He couldn't enjoy breakfast, all these terrible feelings led up until he stood at the edge of the plane. But the very second that he jumped and was gliding in the air, something happened, the fear slowly dissipated and all he could feel was pure bliss! Will Smith has a very important message in this story, he says all that fear was unnecessary. There was no actual reason to be scared all along, it was a waste of stress and anxiety. The reality is, that all the best things in life, are placed on the other side of fear! The wonderful things you want are just right there for you, it's all within reach! The limitation of fear is the invisible wall you made up for yourself, as a wedge between you and the very thing you want.

Henry Ford said, "One of the greatest discoveries a man makes, one of his great surprises, is to find he can do what he was afraid he couldn't do." Have you ever experienced this growing up? You were terrified to do something whether it was due to lack of confidence or lack of knowledge, but once you just did it, you came out on the other side to a remarkable realization that *oh my god, I can't believe I did it*? It's an incredible thing, but for some reason, we're often selling ourselves short at first. Understand this, our spirits and what lies within us, are capable of so much more than what we even know! With knowing this, without limit in your mind, imagine what more you can do.

Both Will Smith and Henry Ford's messages

are very powerful perspectives. Fear is unnecessary and our realization that we are capable of so much more than what we've limited ourselves to, is a game-changer. We screw ourselves out of doing things, we think and think and allow fear to mess up opportunities all the time! It is a choice we make, assumptions of terrible outcomes, that we have no real way of knowing are going to turn out in the first place. We need to take a real look at ourselves and ask what role fear has played in our lives!

Let's say some of the best creators in this world allowed fear to dominate decisions for them, let's be real, we wouldn't have any of their great creations to enjoy today! Think of Steve Jobs, Oprah Winfrey, Thomas Edison, if they assumed the results of things before they even tried and gave in, then we wouldn't have any of their creations to enjoy. Dare to have the self-confidence in yourself to ask the person out, apply for the position, and put your work out there for the world to see. If things don't work out, you'll spend your life living with lessons from the things you tried, versus living with regret on all the things you never tried. I'll even go as far as to say, failing at the things we dared to try in the first place, has a hidden beauty in it, it builds us. And the best-case scenario, if things do work out, you get everything you've dreamed of! There you are, once you weigh out the worst and best-case scenarios the risks involved are worth it, don't you think? From this moment going forward, have the courage to ask yourself if you are allowing fear to dominate you, if it contributes to some of the reasons you are where you are right now.

All you knew, all your life

Society and our upbringing have programmed us to stick with what is safe. Being raised in a household of immigrant parents from Laos, fear dominated my parent's all the time. My mother always said if I didn't learn how to cook, no one would marry me and that if we didn't go to college, we wouldn't get jobs. They instilled fear in us because, in all honesty, they were the ones who were afraid so they projected that on their children. But applying the concepts we discussed before (making assumptions on outcomes that we don't know for certain about), it isn't true that men won't marry you if you're a bad cook. I know women who believe me, wouldn't be caught dead in a damn kitchen and they got a man to put a ring on it! Also, it turns out some of the most wildly successful people in the world, didn't finish college let alone attend! We all have different journeys and possibilities in life. Your parents mean well, they tell you things so they can place you in better circumstances for better outcomes, just in case! Just to be safe! Respect it, but recognize it for what it is. Knowing how to cook is an excellent skill to feed your family right and having a degree sets you up for different opportunities, that is all. But remember, you create you at the end of the day.

Although I hate to admit it, as I got older fear spilled into my adulthood! I found myself staying in relationships with men that I had no business staying with, out of fear of being alone. I buried myself in student loans to pull off my MBA, out of fear that I couldn't get a good job without one. And once I *did* get an okay job after all that commitment to school, I felt afraid to leave it. But what I came to realize is, the fear of being unmarried in my 30's, doesn't mean I should be settling for any deadbeat guy! And just because I worked super hard in college to lead me to an unfulfilling finance job, doesn't mean I should let fear keep me stuck there! I could pursue things outside of my job and fulfill my passion to write! Fear once had a hold on me and motivated a lot of my life decisions, but once I completely let go of feeling afraid to be alone and feeling afraid to do anything other than my office job, it was freeing! In life, it's all dependent on what you allow.

When Fears Come True

I've met some amazing people, who've overcome fears and took a shot at what they loved. When their worst fears came true and it didn't work out the way they had hoped for, do you know what happened? Did they lay down and die over it? No! In fact, in the long run, if they understood the lessons gained and grew from it, then they were still glad they did it. Because the moment they decided fear was not going to dictate them, they felt free and unrestricted.

It enlightened them to the realization that taking risks, allowed them to do things they once thought they were never capable of. And it even opened doors for other opportunities they had not considered, the experience brought them to the right people for the next step. It's a blessing in disguise. The book *The Secret by Rhonda Byrne*, taught us years ago, that once you believe in yourself the universe will begin to move people and circumstances to allow the right things to come to you. So have unwavering trust, even when things don't pan out exactly how you envisioned it to, it's still the best policy to live by at the end of the day.

A personal story of when one of my worst fears came true, is when I worked for a trading company that required getting a license to become a stockbroker. I had to study 90 days for an exam called the Series 7 and it turned out to be the biggest lesson of my life. After putting my absolute all into it I failed the exam, so they gave me another 30 days to pull myself together and retake it. Guess what happened, the guy I was dating at the time broke things off and came clean that he still loved his ex-girlfriend (talk about not giving two shits about timing). So there I was, both heartbroken and trying to study for my retake exam at the same time. Those 30 days were filled with crying all night, no sleep, no food and abusing caffeine to read material day in and day out. When it came time for me to go back in, I did better, but I still failed the test the second time! I was devastated and so afraid of what that failure meant. To me, the failure meant that I was incapable of learning something and getting licensed. It meant that not only was I too stupid to pass a test (twice!), but I couldn't even keep the guy I was dating, interested enough to stay. Then, a friend of mine who passed the exam and remained at the company, said it was terrible working there. She said everyone hated it, clients call in back-to-back to discuss trading options, while you sit in your cubicle. Furthermore, 8 months later, everyone from the trading company got laid off and they were bought out! When I look back on this story, I commend myself for not letting fear prevent me from trying in the first place. I tried and although I failed, I realized in my heart my calling wasn’t to become a stockbroker. I learned that when your emotional and mental state collide, it can be life-changing. But the universe put circumstances into my life to block me from receiving what wasn't meant for me. It turned out to be a blessing that I didn't pass and stay, because it opened me up for other opportunities and overtime I was able to find my real passions. I stopped allowing the fear of looking like a failure, defeat my spirit. These days, I am no longer embarrassed about failing, in fact if I had passed and stayed, I would've been miserable for 8 months and then got laid off anyway! I also wouldn't have found what I have now. Failing didn't represent me as a loser, it represented me as courageous and the experience built me. My fearlessness meant that for one, I was not allowing it to stop me from trying and two, I was not allowing the results of that stupid test to define me. Just know that even if the worst happens, if what you fear will happen comes true, you gain something regardless. When you are courageous, it will result in realizing things about yourself, that you never would have.

Understand fear for what it is, it's self-sabotaging, an outcome of a false conclusion we made up in our minds and is instilled upon us from our upbringing, but our job is to keep that in check and take chances in life. When you're at a crossroads, ask yourself is this appropriate to be afraid of? And what are the true consequences of it? Because the risk might be worth it. The restrictions of fear are destructive to someone's ability to live to their fullest potential. I want you to live to your absolute fullest potential, it's never too late. If you are content with where you are, so be it, if you want more, then go get it! Either way, this life must be spent with you knowing you're being your absolute best and happiest, that's all I ever want to share with you. And although, you will not be able to change the fear-based decisions of your past, call yourself out on your fears from now on. Be aware that it can control you and use that awareness to take charge of your destiny. Be Fearless.

Chapter 2

Be about your Blessings

"A bucket can't catch rain if it's upside down, just like a mind can't catch any lessons or blessings if it stays closed."
-Humble The Poet

Can you remember the last time you counted your blessings? The last time you went through a list in your head, of all the things you earned and gained up to this present moment? We're always obsessing about the things we don't have right now, rather than what we do, that the blessings become harder and harder to see. When I look back on my life, I spent a lot of time thinking I didn't have enough. I would finish college, land a promotion at work and get my first home. Everyone would say, "Congratulations! What an achievement!" right to my face, but I never felt the gratification. I went on for a decade, shaming myself for all the things I still *didn't have.* In my head, ashamed that I wasn't married yet or I wasn't making more money. My head was closed, I didn't see any blessings at all, I was always convinced that I was without something. It is this ongoing torture we can put ourselves through where nothing is enough, even after we reach a milestone, we just focus on a new thing we're without. Leading a life where you accomplish things, but you do not take the time to absorb, to learn and reflect on anything you've gained, is not the path to take. Anything you take on, must be treated like food, digest it, gain from it, grow from it and receive your blessings.

If there's one thing I learned, you will get nowhere when you go about life with the mindset of, *I don't have this, I don't have that, I'll never have.* Because you created a fixed belief in yourself, that you are always without! You screwed yourself into this belief, so-much-so, that one day you could wake up and have a whole lot, but you're still hating your life! Nothing is good enough for you, because you're blind. Remember that no matter how bad you think you have it, there is someone out there who would trade places with you in a hot second. This thing called life is no game, it's not over until it's over. I encourage you to open up your mind, when you are ungrateful, you are blind to all the wonderful things you have in the present. What a shame, because you're missing out. You're missing out on all the people who love you and missing out on all your opportunities, most importantly you're blocking any more blessings from coming to you, every damn day! It's not worth it to live with this mindset.

You have to count your blessings. It is critical that you practice counting all the things you're thankful for, to the point where it trumps your old mindset, of *not enough* and *always without*. Know your blessings to the point where it's all you tell yourself before you go to bed every night, until it becomes a religion to you.

The mind is one of the most powerful tools in our lives, the moment you've managed your thoughts for all you're grateful for, everything slowly shifts for you. You start falling in love with the journey, every single one you embark on. You find hidden gems along your path, things you never took notice of before! It turns out, my blessings weren't in the college degree, the house, the career; but in the rewarding projects and friendships I made while earning my degree. It was in the empowerment I gained, going to my first-time homebuyer's class and signing my closing paperwork, after all I endured to get my first home. Late nights I spent watching YouTube videos to teach myself coding tricks, building my first blog. Even all the rejection I got from the stories I pitched as a freelancer, was a blessing, because It meant they were listening. It humbled me and taught me what publishers want and look for, to be a better writer. You see, the second your mindset becomes about blessings rather than the things *you lack*, you find joy and fulfillment in the pieces of the puzzle it took to get your end goal. It's the little wins that are victories, *it's the little things that count!* The beauty is so much more in the journey than it is in the end goal. If you're only in it for the end goal, it will feel cheap and less satisfying. You'll come up short, you didn't see the blessings along the path to get there and all you had gained along the way, so when you're done you just find yourself searching for the next thing to do! Take a pause, be conscious enough to notice all that you got out of the experience, embrace each step along the way, not just the top of it. After all, it's the journey that transformed you, not the finish line. Does that make sense?

Perspective

Let's say you commit to doing your first triathlon. There's a process ahead, you've created a regime on a specific time when you train every week. You've hit some challenges with your body, made a change to your diet. You feel tired, but you push through it. You've done some more reading on potential risks involved, even met a couple of new friends doing the same race! You go shopping to find the perfect gear, time gets closer and the anticipation sinks in. Finally, the day comes, you start and complete your first race! Suddenly, you're overcome with emotion and it's not just because you finished it, it was all the phases you took to get there. Someone who counts their blessings would look at all they embarked on and see the things they have gained in the weeks that led up to completing the goal. What they learned about their body, spirit, capabilities and new friends, those are the blessings gained along the way. It is most gratifying when you are appreciative of all the things that came to you during the process, all that you got out of it. The moment becomes precious to you, not only because of the victory of completion, but all the transformation that took place for you to get there. Now let's put this in perspective of the mindset of *not enough*. You went through the same thing, the training, the diet, fatigue, shopping, finish line. When you're done, you're overcome with emotion. You're not satisfied, but annoyed. Sure you finished, but you didn't hit the time you wanted to hit. You're thinking back at how much you endured, the pain, the energy, what a waste! What was it all for? What was the point? Your friends say "Congratulations!", they know you committed a lot of hard work to do this triathlon. But it's not enough, you can't even hear them, you don't feel any gratitude. This right here is the difference. You're all about the result rather than the journey, so how can anything good come from a mindset of *not enoug*h? Where even once you finish goals, you don't feel happy.

I was in a relationship with a man who created woodwork in his garage (yes the same guy in chapter one). He gave his woodwork pieces as gifts for friends and family, one day I said: "You know, what if we got your work out there for the community to see?" I was determined, so I worked on getting the pieces hung up under the Local Artist wall display of a small business at 2 store locations in Denver. He sold 4 pieces over 2 months. Each piece that sold, made me jump for joy and say, "Isn't this wonderful?! Your work is getting out there, strangers are buying your work!" But I remember his response, each piece we sold he would say, "Yeah, that's cool. It's just one piece though... that's nothing." He was *never grateful*, never excited. He constantly thought about how it was not enough. A few months passed, and a woman who worked at another business down the street, noticed the pieces and reached out to me for an order of 10 new ones to carry at her store! You see everyone begins small, but those small steps open doors for the next big opportunity. He didn't know how to be about his blessings, he was so ungrateful that he wouldn't see a blessing even if it smacked him in the face. In fact, in the end, when it came time to fulfill the order for 10 signs at the new store, he sabotaged the entire opportunity! True story.

When you're a blessing counter, you're conscious enough to be in it for the experiences. You have an understanding that you're always full, you're fortunate and always gaining. With this enlightened view, you're humbled and you start to change to become a person who sees opportunities, rather than limitations. You change to become a person that knows, any victory (small or big), is a step closer to your end goals and you don't let it discourage you, you are grateful.

We're up against a lot right now with social media, you see people traveling all over the world, drop-dead gorgeous moms in the best shape of their lives, and public figures posing in front of their Maserati's. People want the quick results, they fantasize about the success, because of what they see on social media. The access of social media shoves it in our face all day long. A reminder that this is what they have and what we don't have. You're thinking, Amber how can I count my blessings in this environment? Well first off, if you are a blessing counter, that social media feed wouldn't affect you in this way. Someone who understands their blessings, also understands that success never looks the same in comparison to the next guy, everyone's path is different. You would genuinely love every photo, applaud those who are reaching all their goals and are living their happiest lives! Real Queens applaud other Queens. But if you are the type of person who is with an *always without mindset*, when you see this all over your feed, it will make you feel like shit. You'll be negative and judgmental of them. The comparison of their progress over yours will be damaging. These photos in the feed will make you feel inadequate, that you don't have what they do.

Understand this, every single person on social media began with zero followers, every person came from a different journey and took a different path, but all of us have blessings nonetheless. No one is posting the rejection letters they got from companies they once applied for, the bad reviews they got from disgruntled clients they helped, the nights they cried themselves to sleep when they lost all hope. You don't see all the ups and downs of their journey (or should I say all the downs), you are just seeing the finished product. Be conscious enough to know social media for what it is, we only reveal glamorous parts of us. The fun, adventurous, happy, explorative, party going, high achieving- sides. Don't treat it as a comparison tool, but instead treat it as something resourceful, informative and fun to look at. Additionally, be thoughtful about who you *choose* to follow. Are the people you choose to follow in line with who you are and do they inspire you to be *your* best? If not, then unfollow! Don't let social media rush you to be further along than where you are right now and don't let it negatively impact you.

I know it can seem nearly impossible to find blessings when you're under harder life circumstances. For instance, you were raised in a poor household, limited or have physical ailments. There is a decision that needs to be made, do you still have blessings? Or are you always without? A quote by Stephen Covey, "I am not a product of my circumstances, I am a product of my decisions." I remember watching a story about someone with cancer, she had a remarkable way of mastering her mindset. Despite being told she had a limited time here, she had such a beautiful approach to life. Choosing to spend precious time with family and good friends, counting her blessings and making the most of her journey that's left. Those with life-threatening illnesses are faced with a decision on how they're going to spend the rest of their lives, what's even more inspiring is when they choose to make the most of their days and count their blessings. Don't be that person, who needs a time stamp on their last days on earth, before you start to count your blessings. In a sense, all of our time is going to be up, isn't it? The time to make the most of our journey and to count all the blessings we have gained, is now and every day going forward.

If there's anyone who can understand and respect tough life circumstances it's my family. You see, when my parents and older sister came here from a refugee camp in Southeast Asia, they didn't know a word of English and my dad had $10 in his pocket. Can you imagine having to leave your country into an unfamiliar place, for safety? There's no job lined up for you, you don't know anybody and you can't even speak the language! The Christian family in Seattle who sponsored us, never met us, so everyone was taking risks on both sides. Even with those circumstances, we made it... my parents today still reside in the same house I was raised in, the one they bought in Colorado. And all three of my siblings and I have steady jobs and homes of our own! I mean, my parents cleaned floors and toilets for nearly 25 years, they didn't have a glamorous job and guess what? They came up! They didn't bitch or dwell, they were blessing counters, making the most of what they were handed. Life is like being handed a deck of cards, you were dealt with whatever you're given and what you do with it, is entirely up to you. They took us on whatever little trips they could, were able to feed us every day, had a stable home in order to allow us to focus on our education, and an active social life with friends. My mom always saved up to have her guilty pleasures, high-end purses! We were forever blessed for all we gained in the journey. We all have something to be blessed about, no matter how much money we came from or where, because you build this life any way you want it.

If you have a dream, but don't know how to start, you cannot just lay down and say, "Oh well, I don't know how to do it, so I just can't". No! Take that as your opportunity to find out how to take chances and use your mind to get there, you'll count them as blessings down the road. Right now, we are fortunate to live in a time with so much access to learn how to do anything! Whether it's podcasts, videos, blogs, and social media; the information is all at our fingertips. You can even learn how to change your flat tire with YouTube now (trust me I know)! Sky's the limit.

When we become blessing counters, we start to speak a different language. Something amazing happens, there are no longer notions of, "I can't" instead it turns into, "Sounds like a good opportunity! I want to try and find out how!". It's a beautiful thing once we know that meaningful things lie in what we gain along the way, that's when we stop doing it only for the result and become unstoppable. You'll want to try everything your heart desires, because you know that even if you don't finish to the end, even if you don't make it... it'll still be worth it. You're going to be gaining all these lessons and blessings in the process, regardless of how it turns out!

In life, we get this one shot! You're not a cat, you don't get 9 lives to try this over and over again! Shift your perspectives now for the good. Nothing moves or happens for you without putting forth the appropriate mindset towards it. Just look at the word *pay attention...* The word *pay* is in it, you are paying for that experience, it's costing you something! With this viewpoint, how do you want to spend? Be about your blessings.

Chapter 3

Be Purposeful

"What am I living for and what am I dying for are the same question."
-Margaret Atwood

Do all of the things you commit to align with your bigger picture? Are the groups you're apart of and projects you're working on, getting you closer to your ultimate end goal? If the answer is no, then why do it? It is so easy to get wrapped up in all the tasks you've agreed to do, that one day you realize you bit off way more than you can chew, or even worse, you're working on things that you don't even need to be working on! Have you ever experienced it? One day you're burnt out and asking yourself, "Why the hell did I agree to this shit?!"

Be purposeful, everything that you do has to be in line with where you're trying to be. You have to check yourself, *what* are you doing and *why* you're doing it? If you cannot answer those questions, it's time to re-evaluate. Some of my friends have asked me why are you doing this and why are you so busy with that? I'm certain of my reasons, all of the meet-ups, events and workshops I'm running around for, are things that will help me grow and better myself as a writer and blogger. Everything I do is on purpose! Ensure that everything you do is on purpose.

When I agreed to write an article about a new hiking trail build that the city had been anticipating for many years, the results were 3-fold:

1) The publisher got a fresh new interesting article for their readers to enjoy.

2) I got to build my portfolio and gain more exposure as a writer.

3) The city and its volunteers got a lot of positive buzz and recognition for their hard work.

These results are win-win outcomes that are all on purpose! We planned it this way, we were purposeful about putting a new article out there, all of us with our own end goal in mind. What's even more amazing is the sense that you're helping other people, while they're helping you too. We aren't out here, aimlessly doing shit just to do shit. If everyone in the equation is gaining something for the better, then this is what being purposeful is all about. It is all in line with what the publisher of the article needs, it is all in line with my bigger picture and ultimate end goal of becoming a super writer and it is all in line with how the city wants to celebrate their hard work and accomplishments. I won't do anything if I know it doesn't help me towards my ultimate end goal. Do things that are stepping stones, to get you closer to what you want! Because I assure you, people who aspire to be musical artists, actors, lawyers, doctors, do their research to find out what steps they need to take (List a,b,c,d) and are taking small steps towards getting them there. People aren't out there taking advanced web design classes if they're aspiring to be a nurse! That practice isn't purposeful. Live with intent, everything you do has to be for reason.

Learn how to say No

It's hard as hell to say no to certain things, but believe me, you must say no to the things that you shouldn't be doing; Just as much as you should be saying yes to all the things you should be doing. Let's be honest, many of us have a habit of constantly people-pleasing. Those obligated situations feel the worst, don't they? No good comes of it, because you're doing all these things just to make others happy instead of doing it out of pure love and desire. Let me tell you, over time when you keep saying yes to the things you don't genuinely want to do, you'll start resenting those who ask you. When in all honesty, it's *your fault* you keep agreeing to it in the first place and now they expect it from you! But you will make yourself sick over doing and doing and doing for others, that the things you need to do for yourself, fall behind at your own cost. Learn how to say no. I'll even take this to a personal level as an example, why do people agree to a friend with benefits situation just to be with the person they want physically, when in their heart they want more than that? And once that friend with benefit's dates other people or falls in love with someone else, while they had you on the side, you get hurt? So tell me, why do you agree to be a part of that? It's absurd to do that to yourself, but I see it all the time. If your ultimate goal is to get married someday, why are you wasting your time and compromising your emotional and physical well-being, for the sake of saying yes to what works for someone else, but doesn't work for you? In another scenario, if you date people who don't want kids and you want kids, what the hell are you doing? What a waste of time! And this goes beyond saying no to people, this also means saying no to *anything at all* that doesn't align with your end goal. You're probably thinking, okay... first, she says do things that align with my end goal. Now she's saying, do not do things that don't align with my end goal. Yes! Exactly, you see how that worked out? that is what it is! And essentially, it's saying the same thing isn't it? Look at the equation:

Does it align with my end goal: yes = do it

Does it align with my end goal: no = don't do it

Refuse to do things that aren't in sync with your visions, things that aren't going to help you be your best self. It's really simple if it's not for you, then you can't afford to take it on. People are going to have all kinds of things that worked for them and they suggest for you, but that's not your life or your path to take. Even if what they did was remarkable, that's great! But that's sacred and unique to them, which makes it irrelevant to you, your path is your own and your experiences are your own. Make choices for you and only you.

"People think focus means saying yes to the thing you've got to focus on. But that's not what it means at all. It means saying no to the hundred other good ideas that there are. You have to pick carefully. I'm actually as proud of the things we haven't done as the things I have done. Innovation is saying no to 1,000 things." Steve Jobs

I don't care if you have to say no to a million things, if it means finding the *one right thing* you say yes to.

Do it at 100%

In the beginning, I made the mistake of thinking that multi-tasking was the best policy, but I was wrong. Turns out, I cannot write my articles at the same time that I'm working in the office; because here's what happens, the article I write won't make sense and I'll do a shitty job at work. So either way, whether it's the freelancing or my day job, something gets compromised! If you're doing a bunch of things at once, you're going to deliver it with mediocre results, your work won't be your very best. And let's face it if your name is going to be on it, don't you want it to be your best? It sounds so elementary, but it is essential to do things one at a time, this ensures that you'll give 100% focus and exceptional results every single time you deliver.

Here's what it looks like, it's boring, but bear with

me:

1) When I walk into the office I sit down and commit to working my 8-hour day

2) I go home, make dinner and sit to have a meal with my daughter.

3) When we're unwinding, we chat about our day then she gets ready and goes to bed.

4) After she goes to bed, I turn my laptop on and work on my articles.

5) On a day where I have an event, I leave work earlier and shift focus on representing the blog at the event.

On the surface, it looks like I'm doing multiple things, being an employee, mom, freelancer, networker, but notice that I am not doing 2 or

3 things at the *same time.* I'm doing one, then leaving it behind and shifting focus onto task number two. This allows me to give 100% to my job, 100% to my daughter, my articles, my collaborations and events. Those special days when there's an event, guess what I'm not even thinking about what needs to get done at the office. That part of my brain shuts off! Even in my personal life, If I'm on a date, I'm not on my phone editing my next blog post! Dating is already hard enough as it is, if I'm present then I'm all in, in whatever I'm doing. "Never half-ass two things, whole ass one thing", Ron Swanson of *Parks and Rec.*

You Don't Have Time

When you live purposefully, it comes with the understanding that time *is* running out. When you are purposeful, you know, that there is NO time! Shit needs to get done and there is no other time like the present. Purposeful people make plans and more importantly, they execute them. It's the difference between saying "Oh well" to, "How the hell can we make this happen!" It's the difference between putting things into action, over talking about them and hoping it will fall into your lap.

For those procrastinators out there, who say they've always wanted their own food truck… "Oh well". Or they've always wondered what it would be like to take scuba diving lessons… "Oh well". The trouble is, they think they have time, they think maybe next year, maybe in a few years, or they say things like, "We'll see". Do you know what's going to happen? Nothing. Nothing at all will happen! The food truck remains a past dream and the scuba diving is something they'll never know in this lifetime. All because they simply didn't, just do it! They think they have all this time to try these things out later and the moment they're curious about it, it ends right there. It never goes any further than that!

Apart of what makes life so beautiful, is that we can choose whatever we want to be- right? We can choose who we want to spend time with, how we want to look, how we want to express ourselves. So with this knowledge, when there's something we've always wanted to try or learn to be, then the only thing stopping us...is US! Everything we want exists already, it is up to us as to whether or not we pursue it! And this idea of time, the idea of next year or someday...well, what if you die in a week? I don't care what it is if you aspire to be a good wife, a badass cook, mom or a designer; if you're purposeful, that plan has to be made with *right now* in mind. Because a year from now, you don't want to look back and say to yourself “Man, if I had just started this last year, I would’ve been closer to my end goal by now”. This is about doing things that align with you, learning how to say no to what doesn’t serve you, doing it at 100%, and thinking with right now in mind. Be Purposeful.

Chapter 4

Be the CEO of your life

"When I loved myself enough, I began leaving whatever wasn't healthy. This meant people, jobs, my own beliefs and habits – anything that kept me small. My judgement called it disloyal. Now I see it as self-loving."
-Kim McMillen

Are you aware of the type of people you surround yourself with? I know this may sound harsh, but stop and take a look at who's around you, because it is necessary. Entertain the possibility that your choice of friends, could be contributing to what's stunting your growth and your ability to glow up.

When it comes to your friendships, I ask that you ensure that their character is in line with yours. You see, if your friends are clowns, you'll act like a clown. If your friends are gossipers, you'll act the same way too. Maybe, in the beginning, they were doing all of the gossiping, but over time, inside jokes developed and you kept getting together, then you started participating in the drama too. Then there are the friends who do drugs, for a while you resisted it, because you're good sticking to your drinks, but if you're going to continue to hang out with them, then believe me you might dabble in some too. We never want to admit that monkey see, monkey do. This implies that we don't make our own decisions for ourselves, but its human nature.

This goes beyond just being a horrible influence on you, these types of friendships will slow you down in life! I lived my life a certain way drinking every weekend and spending time with the same circle of friends for years. It's all we ever did, but as soon as I chose to make changes in my life and chase my passions for outdoor writing and blogging, I learned fast and hard that not everyone in that old circle would be coming with me (regardless of how bad I wanted them to). There's a saying that goes, having friends without ambitions is like being on a diet and hanging out in a donut shop. Sticking to the notion of food, because I mentioned donut shop, have you ever been on a strict diet or cleanse and your friends sabotage you by saying, “Just eat one slice of pizza, it's not going to kill you, just one slice!” or, “It’s just one piece of cake, live a little!” let me tell you something, if your friends got your back, they got your back… that's it. They wouldn’t shove it in your face and tell you to compromise your goals, for what? To make *them* feel better for eating it? Makes no sense, its selfish and rude. I take notice of the friends who say, “Wow, you're doing so good, let me know how it goes, I'm happy for you!” or, “I’m cheering you on, you can do it!”. Observe the differences in the way your friends speak to you when you are trying to do something in your life, whether it be health, school, career, or life goals, you’ll know exactly what I’m talking about. You won't make any moves or get anywhere towards your life goals this way, it would be too difficult to thrive in such a toxic circle.

When your friends are content with where they are at in life and how they spend their time, they won't be understanding or even care about why you are making changes with yours. Maybe even some of your friends never chased their dreams, because they allowed fear to dominate their lives, who knows? But if this is the case, they'll never want to hear anything about yours. Does it serve you to be around this?

Grown-Up Choices

I know that evaluating your circle is not easy, sometimes we stay friends with people out of loyalty. At one point in your life, you had the same interests like going to the club, but as time went on and life changed, you are no longer the same people. You stay in those friendships anyway and when asked why, your answers are, "Because we've known each other forever!". So tell me then, is that all it takes to be your friend? Just knowing you for a long time? You have to have some standards. Treat friends the same way you treat relationships, you won't be with just anybody (I hope), so you shouldn't let just anyone be your friend and a part of your environment. We should naturally be drawn to people who are the most like us right now, maybe as you grew up you were drawn to the experimental people, the club goers, etc. but at this age, if you're growing up, then you may find you have a lot less to talk about with those friends anymore. Don't feel guilty, you're still growing! And your friends will either grow alongside you, having new goals and aspirations as well, or they'll desire to stand still- so be it! But do not slow down or stunt your progress to make them comfortable, because once that happens, you're compromising yourself. You must approach this as, *either you grow with me or I outgrow you.* Period.

If you've ever heard of the saying *you are what you eat*, it is the principle that what you take in is what you become. This saying applies in many other aspects of life too, you are who you hang out with. Those you let into your emotional and mental space, can poison you or help flourish you!

Think of who you associate with... let's say if people talk about me,

"Hey, do you know that girl Amber?"

"Oh yea she hangs out with that one crowd, they drink and party all the time... "

That becomes your reputation now, right? It is for this very reason, I don't build friendships with people who don't match who I am. Including irresponsible moms, leaving their kids with their parents and going to the club every weekend. I also don't hang out with people that want to do drugs every weekend, they don't want anything out of life. Trust me when I say help yourself, don't screw yourself. That's going to look different for everyone, but I want to have an environment of ambitious and accomplished bad-asses, because I'm working to become that myself. I choose to surround myself with those who have an entrepreneurial mindset, they know how to work hard and play hard! I'm challenging you here, to be intentional and choosy of your space, your circles and who you spend your time with.

When someone is in your life, regardless of if we're talking lovers or friends, it's because you're allowing it. You chose it! You choose who you're sleeping with, eating with and dedicating your time to. Just as this chapter's quote describes, loving yourself means leaving certain people, jobs, and circumstances, that are not healthy. You need the right people because they are occupying time and space in your life. Do you enjoy being around this person, do they bring out the good in you and are they good for you? If not, let them go! Respect yourself, value your own damn time and energy, because if they are gaining something from you, then you need to be gaining something out of the friendship too. I'm not talking monetary things, I'm talking support and bringing out the best in

I See How You Are

Often you are going to find true friends come to light, in some of the hardest times of your life or in moments when you need them the most. It still shocks me to this day, people are so quick to buy pricey sneakers, high-end makeup and products from celebrities and influencers.

But the moment their friend begins selling a product or has a small business, they're hesitant! Why? They drop all this money on stranger's products all day long, but for their friends, they suddenly become penny pinchers. How can this be? If we love and believe in our friends, we should be their biggest cheerleaders, not become skeptical! You put a product out there and somehow the questions become, "Hmm how much is it? Will you give me a discount since I'm your friend?" Don't fall for this, if your friends know the value in what you do and respect you, they'll buy it at full price or they'll simply say to you, "I'm sorry I can't buy any right now, but let me know how I can help get the word out!" When I came out with my Colorado outdoor blog and had my first publication in a local magazine here in Denver, a girlfriend of mine threw a celebratory party for me. She called our mutual friends to invite them, but no one showed up! It was hurtful, in all the birthdays and occasions I had spent to celebrate these people, I finally had this exciting endeavor for me that no one wanted to congratulate me on. People will show their ass, believe me, it's in the moments when you're growing or changing.

It's increasingly harder to recognize toxic friends when you have been close for so long. Or often you see it, but refuse to address it because the friendship is too valuable to you, so you don't want to make a big deal about it. But this behavior is just a waste of your time, we have to be able to recognize when our friends are doing us wrong.

Goal Sabotager's

There are consequences of hanging onto friendships that compromise your future. If you have a project to work on first thing in the morning that is critical to your life goals, they'll boo you, they'll ridicule you for being stuck up and tell you to get drunk and party with them instead. If for some reason you can't make it to one of their kid's birthday party's, because you fell behind and want to take time to get back on the grind; They'll paint you to be the messed up one, but in all honesty who is in that situation? Their kids will have many more birthdays, but you may not have many more chances to hit the target on your dreams- right? Real friends will be supportive. Let's go through another scenario, say you reach a milestone closer to your life goals. Someone wants to help you record your new song to get out there, well your jerk friends will have zero interest in understanding it or supporting you. Here's the red flag: If these people are noisy and have a lot to say when you're doing bad, but quiet as hell when you are doing good, cut them out of your life, immediately. This only serves to damage your self-esteem and even worse, it will get you wondering, *Am I doing the right thing pursuing my dreams in the first place?* Doubting yourself, because their behavior is wrong and puts your future at risk.

Here is what it looks like to have a healthier environment of friends. If you choose friends who have done similar things that you aspire to do someday for yourself; this is healthy. If you choose friends who want growth, change and good for themselves in their own lives; this is a good sign. These are the friends who will not only root you on, but they'll share ideas in good company. And if they have completely different life goals, that's ok, they respect you for having yours. There will be no way they guilt you for hustling. They don't spend their free time gossiping, but they spend their days discussing exciting projects and ideas you all have! I promise you, the difference is day and night. They'll challenge you, bring out the best parts of you and support you, this is the most valuable type of friendships to have.

Hire Fire Promote

It will not be a comfortable process at first, but once you figure out who you need to cut out of your life and who stays, it will do you a lot of good. I assure you, that being friends with 15 fake people is a lot lonelier than being friends with 3 genuine people, whose character is in line with yours. Wakeup, control your environment, just like a CEO, hire, fire and promote. The type of people you allow in your life will make a world of difference to your happiness.

Be aware of who your friends are, make sure those relationships serve you. Are they healthy additions to your life and your happiness or are they slowing you down? Be the CEO of your life.

Chapter 5

Be About Yourself

"To love yourself right now, just as you are, is to give yourself heaven. Don't wait until you die. If you wait, you die now. If you love, you live now."
-Alan Cohen

We hear it all the time, "Love Yourself", "You have to love yourself!", but what does loving yourself mean? Well, a big part of what it means is that you don't tolerate unacceptable treatment and you understand that being 100% about yourself, allows you to be 100% for others. You've got to understand that in this lifetime, self-love is the foundation of everything. Unless you've established and continue to foster self-love, I promise you will not have solid ground to stand on to handle anything hard in life that comes your way. You can't even change or evolve the appropriate ways, without it. That's just what it is.

Unacceptable treatment, if people in your life speak down on you, habitually harm you or disrespect you as a person… when you love yourself, you'll walk the hell away. When you love yourself, you don't allow them the time of day.

The second you see it, you don't even let a relationship with that person go any further. It has a lot to do with self-respect. I'll use a mild example, I was with someone for 5 years, this person would never commit to me. If it were up to him, he would be content dating me until we died. In those 5 years, I watched him get his apartment, he watched me finish college, we lived separate lives. We loved each other and spent a ton of time together, but he only wanted me in his space at his convenience. I'd go over to his place and cook dinner whenever he wanted, we'd watch a movie and go to bed with one another, only for me to leave the next morning and come back to do it all over again. I wasn't allowed to leave any of my belongings there, if my toothbrush was there, he'd put it away in the drawer every time I left. I had no place in his life, I knew that what he was offering me wasn't in line with what I wanted. And that if I loved myself, I had to accept our differences and leave. If I loved myself, I wouldn't force myself to stay in a relationship that only serves him and doesn't serve me. The thing is in those 5 years, I saw no progression, but I loved him more than I loved myself and I also had a fear of being alone (remember chapter one). Which allowed me to stay longer than I should have.

Being 100% about yourself results in being the best for others, you cannot pour from an empty cup. For a long time, I believed that giving and giving is what makes us a good person. In truth, it's not worth a damn thing, hear me out... if you're giving all the time, but at the end of the day feel resentful, sad, under-appreciated and unloved, somethings wrong with that formula. What needs to occur, is your ability to take care of yourself wholly and completely first, before any giving can occur. Fill your cup up and you can be the best for others, because you are not doing right by those you love when you're empty. Just think about how much better of a spouse, parent or friend you would be if you just took care of yourself first? It's like going to work on a full stomach and full night's sleep. When I haven't tended to myself or when I'm going through something, I will tell my friends, "Sorry I'm dealing with something right now and I can't be a good friend until I handle this first. I love you." Look, when an airplane is about to crash the instructions are to put your breathing mask on first, before you put the breathing mask on your babies. Why? Because if you put it on your babies first and pass out, you are no good at helping anyone at that point then- are you?

I hold the lesson of self-love so high, because I didn't have it or know how to have it in my entire 20's. I let a lot of people do a lot of things to me. I became all about the comfort of others and what they needed from me. Every year, my friends and I would have a friend's Christmas party. Here's how it went down, all of the adults bought gifts for each other's kids. I have one daughter, however, each of my friends in the group had 2-3 kids. I found myself dishing hundreds and hundreds of dollars on this friend's Christmas party and spending barely any money for my own Christmas! And get this, sometimes, my friends would even *forget* the one gift they had to get for my daughter! And remember I have just one kid! I didn't have my priorities straight, it was all wrong for me. How can I justify spending $400-$500 for this ridiculous friends Christmas party every year, when some of my friends were forgetting to even get my daughter something? How can I justify spending more on my friend's multiple kids over spending on my own mom, dad, brother, sister and own daughter? Furthermore, I'd spoil my friends on their birthdays and then once my birthday came up, often times I wouldn't even get a text message! Stand up for yourself and for what's right, because things like this aren't okay. This is not about expectations, it's not about *I bought you this, so you need to buy me that.* Expectations are the wrong thing to have, this is more about looking at what kind of people you're spending your time, money and energy on. I was doing this for so long that I woke up one day and didn't know who the hell I was! With men and friends, I didn't know what I was doing or why! It's a traumatic awakening, to be at your lowest of low, realize you have a phony boyfriend and friends, and have to learn how to start all over again! To try and find out who you are, being all grown at 32.

If self-love and self-respect were taught to me much sooner as a young woman, maybe I would've held myself to a higher priority. Today,

I don't even blame people for how they are. Because at the end of the day, I have to take accountability for what I allowed. And maybe with self-love, when people left, I would've freely allowed them to, without taking insult. Maybe I could've been a person that gave more genuinely, rather than out of obligation. Maybe, if I was a better person to myself, I could've also been for those I loved. It's never too late to take care of yourself, it's a forever maintenance we have to do.

Putting it all together

The prior chapters discussed here need self-love, to put into action:

1) Being Fearless - If you do not love yourself. You will not value yourself enough to listen to you inner conscience. In turn, you will not have the ability to understand how fear is shaping you. Having the courage to not let fear control your decisions, requires

that you listen to whats going on inside of you and that you know you're worth taking chances on.

2) Counting Your Blessings - If you don't love yourself. You are convinced that you are not deserving of anything good. So you are blind to any of the good you have received even once you have received it. You are not awake! You're oblivious, therefore you cannot possibly see any of your blessings.

3) Living With Purpose - You commit to things even when they are not in line with your end goal, even when they compromise you. Because your priority is making others happy over yourself. You always say yes, even when it has no purpose for you, no matter the cost.

4) Controlling Your Circle - You won't value yourself enough to create a healthier environment of people around you. You allow freinds and lovers who do not respect or love you properly, to be in your life and continue to harm your growth. Hindering your emotional and mental well-being.

Leading a life without self-love prevents you from becoming your best self. How can you expect any change, any evolving and any growth when you haven't laid down the self-love initially to begin with? You won't last, because you'll allow doubt to stop you from doing the things you're most afraid of, you'll do things without appreciation and with an *always without* mindset, you'll do things that provide no purpose, and you'll be around people who don't support you.

If you never give to yourself, you can't even know what you like. You can't know who you are or what you need to work on. Value yourself enough to take the time to figure that out. You'll be surprised when you find out what brings you happiness and what doesn't. There are so many times, when I thought I liked certain things that turns out wasn't me at all. You'll start gaining who you want to become and what it is you need. And something amazing starts to happen, the wrong lovers no longer have a place in your life. You no longer feel hurt, when your friends try to guilt you for things. You do things to please yourself first and organically become the best friend, parent, co-worker, and spouse for others. You become in complete control of what your life looks like.

I promise change can begin to take place once you love yourself. Being fearless, being about your blessings, living with purpose and being the CEO of your life, can properly be put into place. It is about making you and your life the number one priority, with self love comes the possibility of changing to be your best self. It's about owning up to your environment, relationships and your bullshit. It all starts with you, what you value, what you tolerate and what you want for yourself at the end of the day. It's time for transformation, are you ready to Glow Up?

References

Chapter 1: Be Fearless

p.13

Meah, A. *35 Inspirational Suzy Kassem Quotes On Success*. Retrieved from https://www.awakenthegreatnesswithin.com/35-inspirational-suzy-kassem-quotes-on-success/

p.18

Truly Motivational. (2015, March 6). Fear Is Not Real [Web Log Post]. Retrieved from http://www.trulymotivational.com/fear-is-not-real/

p.19

Adventureusla. (2017, April 19). *Will Smith on Skydiving* [Video file]. Retrieved from https://www.youtube.com/watch?v=gG-F_rRVdLc

p.20

Vargas, C. (2014, June 2). *10 Must read quotes from Henry Ford on business & leadership*. Retrieved from https://www.thestudyabroadportal.com/studyabroadblog/10-must-read-quotes-from-henry-ford-on-business-leadership/

p.26

Byrne, R. (2006). *The secret.* New York: Hillsboro, Ore.: Atria Books.

Chapter 2: Be About Your Blessings

p.31

Singh, K. (2019, August 5). @humblethepoet [Web Log Post]. Retrieved from

https://www.humblethepoet.com/blogs/news

p.44

Meier, J.D. Best Steven Covey Quotes [Web Log Post] Retrieved from http://sourcesofinsight.com/stephen-covey-quotes/

Chapter 3: Be Purposeful

p.49

Atwood, M. The Year of The Flood Quotable Quote [Web Log Post]. Retrieved from https://www.goodreads.com/quotes/227870-what-am-i-living-for-and-what-am-i-dying

p.56

Jobs, S. Quotable Quote [Web Log Post]. Retrieved from

https://www.goodreads.com/quotes/629613-people-think-focus-means-saying-yes-to-the-thing-you-ve

p.59

Daniels, G. & Schur, M. (Creators). (2009). *Parks and Recre-*

ation [Television series}. Los Angeles, CA: Deedle-Dee Productions and Universal Media Studios.

Chapter 4: Be The CEO of Your Life

p.63

McMillen, K. When I Loved Myself Enough Quotes [Web Log Post]. Retrieved from https://www.goodreads.com/author/quotes/40853.Kim_McMillen

Chapter 5: Be About Yourself

p.78

Brockway, L.S. 11 Inspiring Quotes About Self Love [Web Log Post]. Retrieved from https://www.huffpost.com/entry/12-inspiring-quotes-about_b_5381155